FAST and EASY
NEEDLEPOINT

D0604671

FAST and EASY NEEDLEPOINT

Mary Anne Hodgson and

Josephine Ruth Paine

Photographs by Michael Pitts and Richard Fowlkes

Doubleday & Company, Inc., Garden City, New York

Library of Congress Cataloging in Publication Data

Hodgson, Mary Anne.
    Fast and easy needlepoint.
    SUMMARY: Uses a series of learning designs to teach the basic needlepoint stitches, then guides the reader into original designs for a belt, pillow, guitar strap, and other objects.
    1. Canvas embroidery—Juvenile literature.
[1. Canvas embroidery. 2. Needlework] I. Paine, Josephine Ruth, joint author. II. Pitts, Michael. III. Fowlkes, Richard. IV. Title.
TT778.C3H63   746.4′4
ISBN 0-385-12431-7 Trade
        0-385-12432-5 Prebound
Library of Congress Catalog Card Number 76–56302

THIS BOOK IS DEDICATED
TO THE YOUNG DESIGNERS
WHO MADE IT POSSIBLE

Contents

What Needlepoint Is

Needlepoint is easy. All you do is cover threads of a stiff canvas with yarn in a big needle. Your needle comes UP through one hole in the canvas and DOWN through a nearby hole. Then your needle comes up and down in neighboring holes, over and over, until the canvas is covered with yarn.

This book shows you how to make ten different needlepoint stitches. If you read Part One very carefully, you can learn without a teacher and make a needlepoint design at the same time. Then do the learning designs in Part Two, in order. After these, you can be a true artist and make your own designs with the ten stitches you have learned.

The needlepoint in this book is very fast to do. We learned this from ten friends who got together one summer when school was out. Within two weeks, they had made these learning designs, knew all ten stitches, and had started on their own designs.

We also sent these directions to friends who lived far away—to Betsy in Alaska, to John in Texas, to Blair in Washington, to Michele and Melissa in Georgia. They learned all by themselves, and they still enjoy needlepoint.

Now it's your turn. Turn the page and do it!

PART ONE

Getting Started

First of all, use the shopping list on the next pages to get the supplies you need at a needlepoint shop. Maybe a good friend who likes crafts projects can shop with you. That way, you can each buy different colors of yarn and share them.

A Note About Measurements

Dimensions are given in inches followed by metric measurements in parentheses. As most people find it much easier to work with round figures, we have used them whenever possible, and, therefore, the centimeter measurements are exact conversions only when they need be.

SHOPPING LIST

ONE HALF YARD (0.5 m) OF NO. 10 MONO CANVAS

All learning designs in this book are planned for this size canvas. *Mono* means the canvas has single threads that crisscross. *No. 10* means that every inch (2.5 cm) of canvas has 10 holes. Later you can try other sizes of canvas with larger or smaller holes.

ONE PACKAGE OF NO. 18 TAPESTRY NEEDLES

These have big eyes and blunt points. No. 18 is the perfect size to take yarn through No. 10 canvas holes. If other sizes are suggested, say "No, thank you."

TAPESTRY YARN IN 5 COLORS

Get 4-ply yarn that comes in 40-yard (36 m) bundles. It is fat enough to fill up the holes of No. 10 canvas. Tapestry yarn looks like knitting wool, but it won't get fuzzy as knitting wool does. Persian yarn, which costs more and which can be divided into strands, is also just right. If you get Persian yarn, do not divide the strands.

Colors: Take your choice from these groups. Try to match the colors you see on the cover of this book.

2 bright HOT colors (strawberry pink, hot pink, orange, or red)
2 bright COOL colors (green and blue)
1 very PALE color (light green or yellow)
1 very DARK color (black or purple)
1 white or off-white

WATERPROOF MARKER WITH GRAY INK

If your needlepoint shop does not have a marker that is guaranteed to be waterproof for marking on canvas, go to an art supply store. Ask for an illustrator's pen or permanent felt-tip pen. To test it, wet a scrap of canvas. Mark on it. Let it dry. If the ink does not run, use that pen to draw designs on both canvas and paper.

You probably already have these things at home:

SMALL SCISSORS WITH POINTED TIPS, for clipping yarn

LARGE SHARP SCISSORS, for cutting canvas

MASKING TAPE ¾ inch (2 cm) wide, for taping canvas edges

PAPER AND PENCIL, for drawing your own designs

SOMETHING TO KEEP EVERYTHING IN—a clear plastic bag or a basket

PINK PUPPY PATTERN

Trace the lines on your canvas.

PINK PUPPY

Upright Gobelin Stitch

Your First Needlepoint Piece

TO BEGIN: Get your canvas ready, like this:

1. From the corner of your canvas, cut a piece 4 inches (10 cm) long and 5 inches (12.5 cm) wide. Measure it with a ruler and mark the cutting line with a pencil first.

2. Place your 4-by-5-inch (10 by 12.5 cm) canvas square right on top of the Pink Puppy pattern. See the black lines peeking through the holes of the canvas? Make sure each straight black line peeks through a straight line of canvas holes. Trace the lines only, onto the canvas, with your waterproof marker.

3. Cover the cut edges of the canvas with masking tape. Mark an X at the top. This will help you remember which is the top of the picture.

NEXT: Cut about 18 inches (46 cm) of bright green yarn. To put the yarn through the needle, follow the pictures.

HOW TO PUT YARN THROUGH A NEEDLE

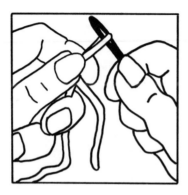

1. Loop the end of the yarn around the needle. Pinch yarn and needle tightly.

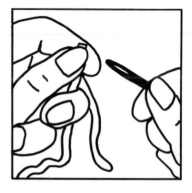

2. Keep pinching the yarn while you pull the needle out.

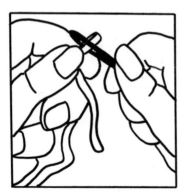

3. Keep pinching the yarn, but open your finger and thumb slightly. When the fold of yarn peeks out, slip the fold through the eye of the needle.

4. Pull a few inches of yarn all the way through the eye to let one end hang free while you make stitches.

Now you are ready to make a simple stitch with a fancy name, the Upright Gobelin Stitch. Like a train, Upright Gobelin Stitch stays on a straight track of canvas threads. It never jumps the track.

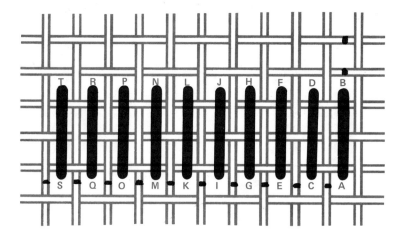

On a chart, a row of Upright Gobelin stitches looks like this.

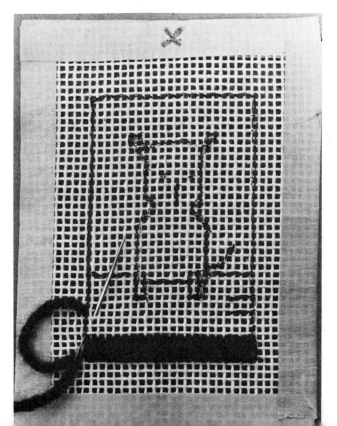

On your canvas, a row of Upright Gobelin stitches will look like this, sitting on the bottom line you drew.

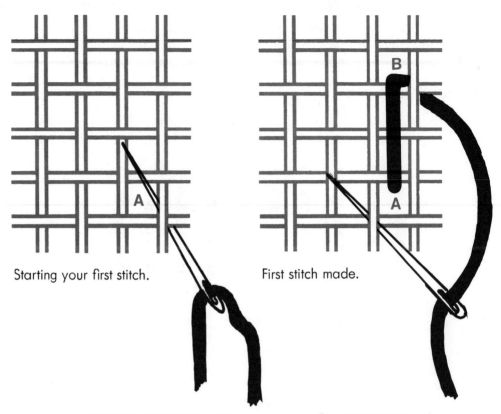

Starting your first stitch.

First stitch made.

FIRST STITCH: Put your needle BEHIND the canvas. Bring it up through the hole marked A on the line at the bottom right-hand corner of the box you drew. Bring your hand around to the front side of the canvas and pull all the yarn through Hole A, except the 1-inch (2.5 cm) tail. Use the index finger of your other hand to hold that tail against the back side of the canvas until other stitches cover and hold it. To finish the stitch, poke the needle into Hole B, 3 canvas threads above Hole A. Pull the yarn all the way through, except the tail you are holding.

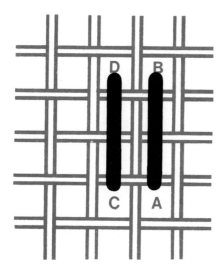

Two stitches made.

SECOND STITCH: Bring the needle up through Hole C, which is 1 canvas thread over from A. Did that stitch catch your finger behind the canvas? Good. You can let the yarn loose, and it will stay in place from now on. Finish this stitch by poking the needle into Hole D, 3 canvas threads above Hole C.

Now you have two Upright Gobelin stitches. Are they fat enough to keep the canvas threads between them hidden? Good. Keep going with Step E–F, Step G–H, to the edge of the small box. It is important that the tops and bottoms of each stitch in this row are very even, running across the canvas in the same track of canvas holes, just as they do in the Upright Gobelin Chart.

WHAT TO DO WHEN YARN TWISTS

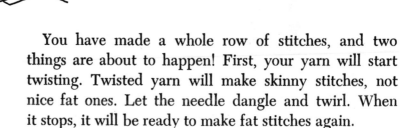

You have made a whole row of stitches, and two things are about to happen! First, your yarn will start twisting. Twisted yarn will make skinny stitches, not nice fat ones. Let the needle dangle and twirl. When it stops, it will be ready to make fat stitches again.

Also, your yarn is getting shorter. When it is about 4 inches (10 cm) long, it is time to bind it off and start with new yarn. Turn the canvas over so you can see the backs of the stitches. Run the needle under a few inches of the tunnel between the canvas and the stitches, then up and out, pulling the yarn smooth. Clip with scissors. Thread your needle again, and keep stitching.

HOW TO END YARN ON BACK OF CANVAS

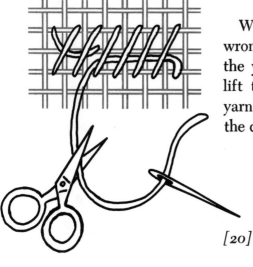

WRONG STITCH: Any time you go through a wrong hole (as everyone does now and then), take the yarn out of the needle. With the tip of the needle, lift the yarn back through the canvas hole. Put the yarn back through the needle's eye. Then go through the correct hole and keep stitching.

[20]

SECOND ROW: Hold your canvas with the front side facing you. Put the X at the bottom. You will make the rest of the grass with the canvas upside down. Make the second row of green grass exactly like the first row. Each stitch goes over 3 canvas threads. In this row, A is 3 canvas threads below the last stitch you made in the first row. B shares a hole with that stitch.

Holding the canvas upside down lets you come UP through an empty hole and DOWN through the shared hole. Stitching is easier this way, and the yarn will not fuzz.

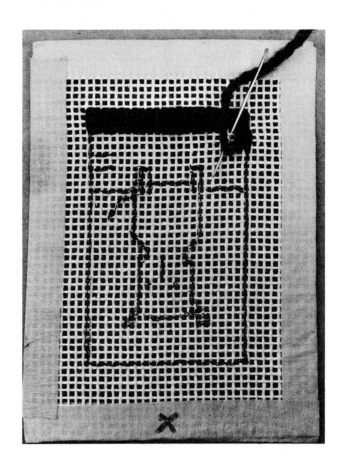

Turn canvas upside down when you stitch second row.

THIRD ROW: One thing is different in this row. Each stitch is short and goes over only TWO threads. It will be another row of green grass. When you get to the end of this row, go into the tunnel on the back and clip the yarn, because you will stitch next in another color. If you have too much green yarn left in the needle to throw away, put the threaded needle aside for later.

TO MAKE THE PUPPY: Thread another needle with about 18 inches (46 cm) of strawberry pink yarn (or orange or red, if you prefer). Keep the X at the bottom. The first line of stitches you will make will be the puppy's legs and bottom. Start at a leg. Begin each stitch 4 canvas threads away from the last row of grass, and end each stitch in the hole it shares with the row of grass. The beginnings of all stitches in this row will start in the same row, but the endings will stay on the bottom line you drew for the puppy. (Later you will fill in the blanks that are left.) Keep the X at the bottom until you finish the puppy.

STOMACH: Make a row of Upright Gobelin stitches, all over 4 threads, running from one side of the puppy to the other.

UPPER BODY: Since the puppy's shoulders slant, the outer stitches of the line will start on the shoulder lines you drew. The middle stitches will start at the puppy's chin. All will share holes with the stomach line.

CHEEKS: Start stitches on the line where you drew the eyes. Skip the place where you drew the nose.

TOP OF HEAD AND EARS: Fill in all the areas that are left in the puppy outline with stitches of different lengths, all running in the same direction as your other stitches.

TAIL: Use short up-and-down stitches to cover the line you drew. If your puppy's tail is wider or wags more than the tail of the puppy in the picture, that's fine. It's your picture, your puppy, and his tail!

NEXT ROW: Puppies don't sit ON the grass; they sit IN the grass. So, on either side of the puppy, make the last row of green grass, over 3 canvas threads. The grass between his legs will be shorter stitches.

EYES AND NOSE: Thread a needle with a short length of black yarn. Make the nose with 1 or 2 long stitches. Pink stitches are covering up the dots you drew for eyes, but you remember where they are. Make 2 SIDEWAYS stitches there.

BACKGROUND: Thread a needle with white or pale yellow yarn. Put the X at the TOP. (Are your hands still clean? If not, wash them or you will have to call this a Dirty Dog picture.) Starting at the top of the picture, make a row of Upright Gobelin stitches. Each stitch will start 3 canvas threads below the top line you drew. Each stitch will end on that top line, all the way across the picture.

SECOND ROW: Keep the X at the top, and keep it there for all the rows that are left to do. The second row starts with stitches over 3 canvas threads, but the puppy's ears will get in the way of some stitches. Make those stitches shorter, sharing bottom holes with ears and top holes with the row you just finished.

ALL OTHER ROWS: In the space to the right of the puppy, fill in all the space, right up to the puppy, with rows of Upright Gobelin stitches over 3 canvas threads. Then make the same rows on the left side of the puppy. The last row of background on each side may be 2 or 3 or 4 canvas threads. It doesn't matter. Just fill in the space that is left.

[24]

FINISHING THE PICTURE: After all the rows are finished, the back of the picture will look shaggy. Clip any long pieces of yarn dangling from the back so that they are about ½ inch (1.3 cm) long.

FRAMING THE PICTURE: Use a standard 5-by-7-inch (12.5 by 18 cm) frame. If you can, choose a frame with glare-proof glass. The mat around the frame can be cut the proper size for you if you take both frame and needlepoint to a framer. Tape the canvas to the back of the mat with masking tape.

You've finished! Now try the stitches and designs, in order, in Part Two.

Back of needlepoint will look shaggy.   Front will look finished.

PART TWO

Seven Learning Designs

If you make the next seven designs in the order they are shown, you will learn one or two new stitches and one or two new tricks with each design. When you have finished, you can make the designs into things to use or wear. Directions for making them into pillows, pictures, belts, straps, hatbands, and pockets are given in Part Four.

In this part, you can spend less time reading and more time stitching, because the Pink Puppy showed you tricks to use in every needlepoint design.

The stitches in the first four designs are up-and-down stitches. They get their names from the way they are grouped on the canvas.

TRICKY FISH

Single Brick Stitch
Double Brick Stitch

Already you can trace a design, start and stop a needleful of yarn, follow a chart, and use a design to create a picture. No way this fish can trick you!

TO BEGIN: Cut canvas 6½ inches (16.5 cm) wide, 6 inches (15 cm) long. When you trace the pattern, make sure the fish's nose and the pinched-in part of his tail are on the same line of canvas holes. Trace the box and the OUTLINE of the fish. The colored marks in his middle are only to show where you put the first line of stitches and do not need to be traced. Tape the canvas edges and put an X at the top.

TRICKY FISH PATTERN

Trace black lines on canvas. Other lines show first row of stitches.

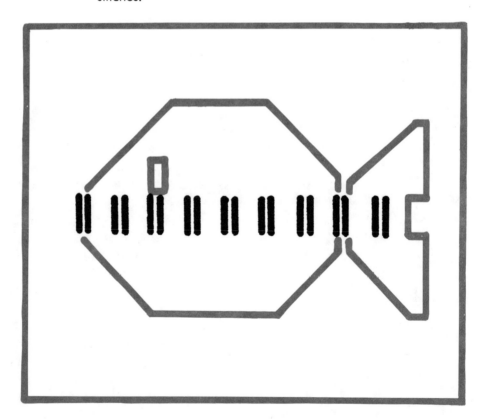

The fish's body is made with groups of TWO up-and-down stitches sitting side by side. Gaps of 2 canvas tracks are left between each group. You fill the gaps as you make the second row of stitches. This is called Double Brick Stitch.

You can make rows of stitches from right to left or from left to right instead of turning the canvas upside down with each row.

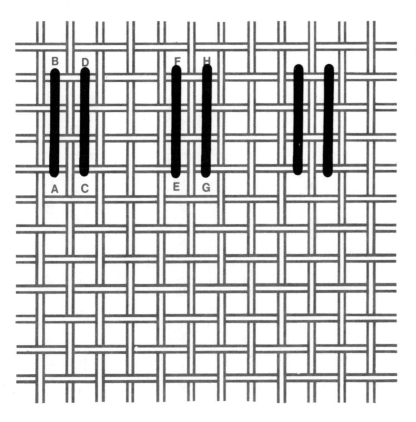

DOUBLE BRICK STITCHES

One row over 4 canvas threads. Skip 2 tracks of threads between each pair of stitches.

[29]

TRICKY'S BODY: Choose 2 HOT colors. With one of them, start the first row on Tricky's nose. Make the row shown on the pattern. Skip TWO tracks of holes between each Double Brick Stitch and the next. Make sure each stitch covers 4 canvas threads. Finish off the yarn at the end of the row, or keep the end out of the way while you do the next row in another color.

SECOND ROW: Use your SECOND hot color. This row fits between the stitches of the first row. It sits 2 canvas threads lower than the first row. Make the same number of Double Bricks you made in the first row. On the chart, the second row is shown in white stitches. Start at a.

Start Row 2 at a–b. See how Row 3 fits in?

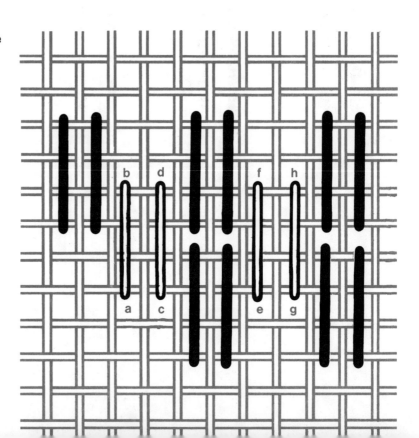

THIRD ROW: Look at Tricky's picture below. See how the first Double Brick in this row fits between the first two bricks of the last row you made? See how the stitches share holes with the first row? Use your FIRST hot color. By making every other row ACROSS in a different color, you are making colored stripes that go up and down. Tricky!

OTHER ROWS: Keep switching colors with each row. The first and last Double Bricks on each row can straddle Tricky's outline until you get to his bottom row.

BOTTOM OF FISH: When you near the outline, there may not be room for a complete Double Brick. Fill the spaces with half bricks to make an even bottom line. Later you can fill the space below the line with background color.

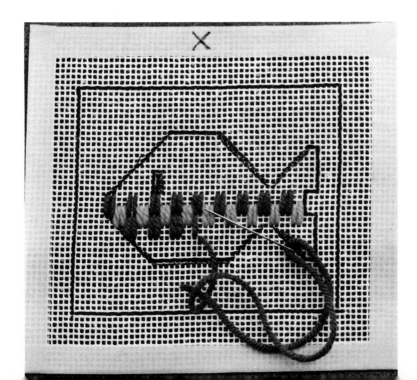

TOP OF FISH: Turn the canvas so that the X is DOWN to make the rows in the top of Tricky's body.

EYE: Did you cover the eye space with a hot color? That's fine. To turn it into an eye, use a cool color. Make 2 stitches close together, right over the stitches that are already in that spot. This makes a fat, bulgy, fishy eye.

TOP LINE OF FISH: To make an even top line, fill with half bricks.

BACKGROUND: This is done in Single Brick Stitch. You make ONE stitch over 4 canvas threads, skip ONE track of canvas, make ANOTHER stitch, skip another track, and keep going. The next row fits between the stitches in this row, 2 canvas threads higher or lower.

SINGLE BRICK
STITCH

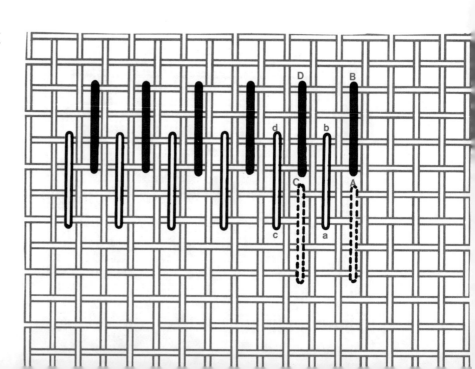

BACKGROUND COLOR: For a solid background, choose ONE cool color. For a striped background, choose TWO cool colors and switch colors with each line. You decide which to make.

TO START THE BACKGROUND: Put the X at the bottom. Make a row of Single Bricks from the middle of Tricky's nose to the front margin of the box. Add the second row between those stitches and let it sit 2 canvas threads lower than the first row.

As you near the fish with each row, there will be spaces too small to use whole stitches. Fill in just the part of the Single Brick you have room for. Soon you will have the space between the front margin and the FRONT of Tricky filled. Then your rows of stitches can go all the way from the front to the back margin.

TO FINISH: When you have filled all the space BELOW Tricky, do the rows behind his tail and the lines ABOVE him. When background stitches are done in this order, rows stay even. Put the X at the top.

Do you like your fish? Then you may want to make others. Try a cool fish in a hot sea, or a solid fish in a solid sea, or add fins. Even though they are small, these fish can be turned into big pillows. Part Four tells you how.

SMOOTH SAILOR
Parisian Stitch

If the wind is right, this boat will move right along. Most of the design is Parisian Stitch. By now you can learn this stitch by looking at the charts. If you want to use another color scheme, fine!

SMOOTH SAILOR PATTERN

Trace all lines on canvas.

TO BEGIN: Trace the pattern on a square of canvas that is 7½ by 7½ inches (19 by 19 cm). With blue yarn, make the top row of sea in one row of Parisian Stitch. Let the row straddle the line of the sea that you drew beneath the boat. Below that row, do another row of Parisian Stitch in green. Stitch with the X at the top. Keep changing colors with each row until you reach the bottom of the box. At the bottom, fill with half stitches to make an even edge.

ONE ROW OF PARISIAN STITCH

To begin, let A–B cover 2 canvas threads. Let C–D cover 4 canvas threads.

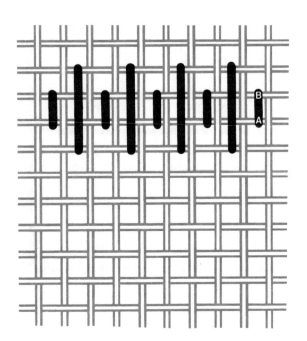

TWO ROWS OF PARISIAN STITCH

In Row 2, let a–b cover 4 canvas threads and c–d cover 2 canvas threads. See how it fits into Row 1? Fit all rows together this way.

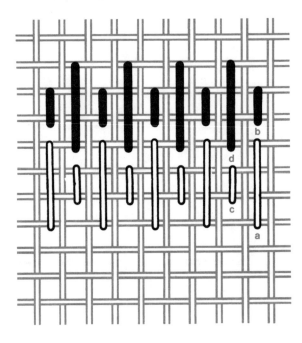

BOAT: Turn your canvas so that the X is down. In red or orange, make the row nearest the sea in Parisian Stitch. As this row fits into the row of sea stitches, the sea stitches look like little waves lapping against the boat. At the top of the boat, fill with half stitches to make an even edge. Wait to make the mast, sail, and pennant.

SAILOR: The sailor's body, in pink, is made of long Gobelin stitches that run along the canvas track from SIDE TO SIDE. They reach from one side of the body outline to the other. To make them, turn the canvas sideways.

HAT: Use blue or green. Make side-to-side Gobelin stitches from one side of the hat outline to the other.

PENNANT: Make side-to-side Gobelin stitches in blue or green.

SAIL: Make Parisian stitches in blue or green.

MAST: Make side-to-side Gobelin stitches over 2 canvas threads. This will make a very straight mast to hold the sail and pennant high above the boat.

BACKGROUND: In yellow or another pale color, make rows of Parisian stitches. Make half stitches to fill out the top edge.

HOT POCKET
Flame Stitch

When you sit by a cozy fire on a cold winter night, you can see how the Flame Stitch got its name. There are many versions and many names for this kind of stitch. Most people call them all Bargello, which is the name of a castle in which chair coverings and wall hangings were made with up-and-down stitches like these.

All stitches go over 4 canvas threads, straight up. Each stitch sits 2 threads higher or 2 threads lower than the stitch beside it. Each row will be a jagged line.

TO BEGIN your pocket (or pincushion, or rug for a dollhouse), cut a square of canvas at least 6¼ by 6¼ inches (16 by 16 cm). In the middle, outline a 4½-by-4½-inch (11.5 by 11.5 cm) box.

CHOOSE COLORS: You will need 2 hot colors (perhaps orange and red) and 2 light colors (perhaps yellow and white).

FIRST ROW: Thread your needle with Light Color no. 1. Start at the RIGHT margin of the box you drew. To find the first hole (A), count 6 threads from the top margin and bring your needle up through the hole below the sixth thread. Now put your needle down into Hole B, 4 threads above Hole A. That is your first stitch.

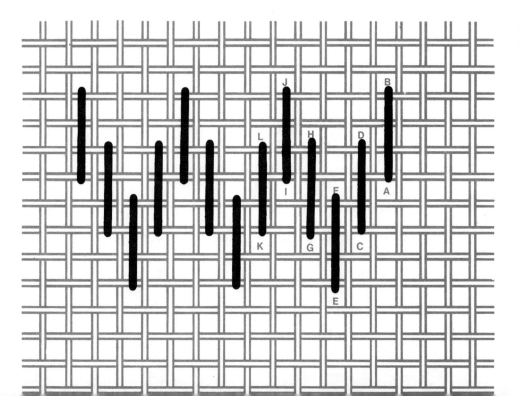

ONE ROW OF FLAME STITCH

SECOND STITCH: Bring your needle up through Hole C, 2 threads below Hole A, but in the next track of holes. Then put your needle down through Hole D.

THIRD STITCH: Let this stitch sit 2 threads below the stitch you just made, in the next track.

CLIMBING STITCHES: Now your stitches begin to climb UP. The fourth stitch begins 2 threads ABOVE the bottom of your last stitch, in the next track. Is it even with that second stitch you made? Good. The fifth stitch brings you back to the top again. It is even with the very first stitch in the line.

To finish the row, think MIDDLE-DOWN-MIDDLE-UP, MIDDLE-DOWN-MIDDLE-UP. Make sure all UP stitches sit on the same line, all MIDDLE stitches sit on the same line, all DOWN stitches sit on the same line.

SECOND ROW: Thread a needle with Light Color no 2. Count FOUR threads below the first step of the row you just made. Bring your needle UP through the hole below the fourth canvas thread. The top of the stitch shares a hole with the stitch in the row above. You can see that this row will be easier than the first one, because the first row is your guide for every stitch. All other stitches start 4 threads below and share a hole with the stitch in the row above.

OTHER ROWS:

Row 3 — Light Color no. 1   Row 7 — Light Color no. 1
Row 4 — Hot Color no. 1   Row 8 — Light Color no. 2
Row 5 — Hot Color no. 2   Row 9 — Light Color no. 1
Row 6 — Hot Color no. 1

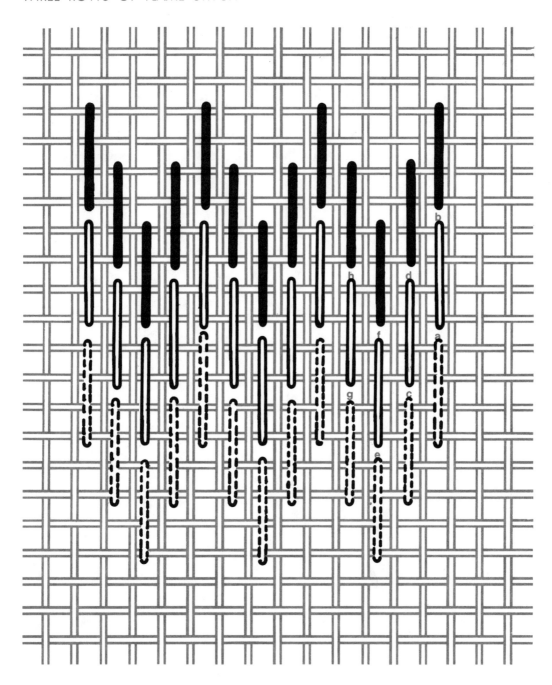

Now you have filled the whole box except the top and bottom edges. Use Hot Color no. 1 or no. 2 to fill the empty spaces with up-and-down stitches that make an even edge. Use 2 stitches to fill the longest tracks.

If your square is to be a pocket for a sweater, for jeans, or for a skirt, make a cloth lining. If it is to be a pincushion, add a back and stuff it. If it is to be a rug for a dollhouse, add a pad. Part Four tells you how.

STRIPS AND STRAPS

Variations of Gobelin Stitch
Back Stitch

You can make all sorts of things with this long, narrow design. For now, let's try a bookmark. Later, if you decide to make a belt, a camera strap, or a guitar strap, you will find the measurements in Part Four. Before you begin, look carefully at the Design Chart on the next page. Make sure you understand how to follow it.

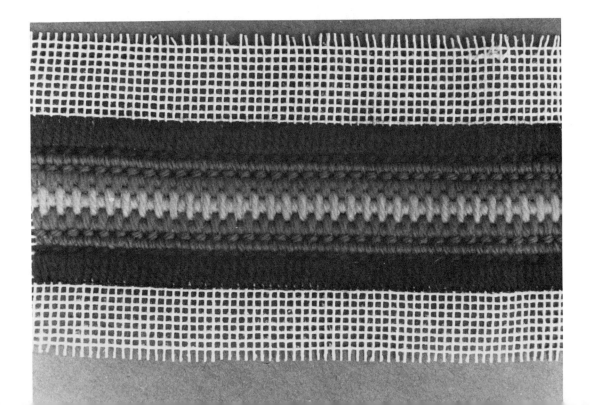

DESIGN CHART

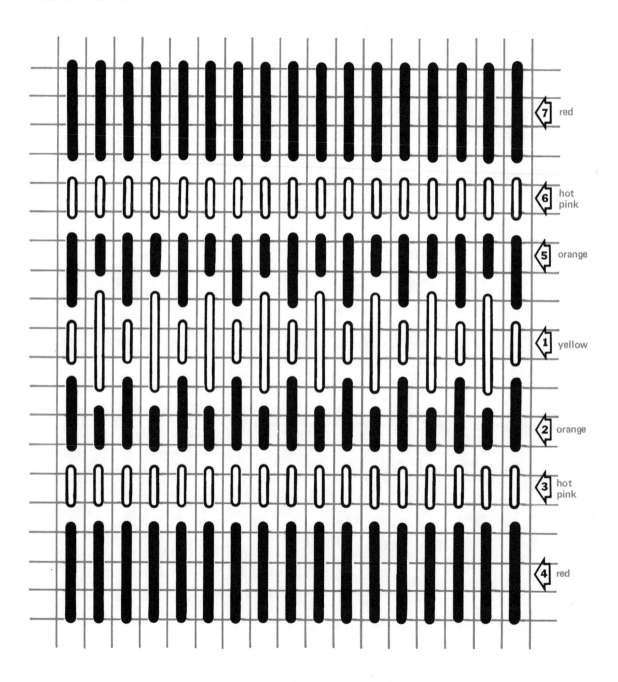

7 red

6 hot pink

5 orange

1 yellow

2 orange

3 hot pink

4 red

Making a Design from a Design Chart

Just as you have learned stitches from a Stitch Chart, you can learn a whole design from a Design Chart. Charts are quicker; you don't need so many words.

This Design Chart shows several stitches and how they fit together. The canvas threads are shown as crisscross lines. The arrows show which row of stitches to make first, second, third, and so on. All rows go from one end of your bookmark to the other. Each row will need more stitches than are drawn on the chart. Longer straps using this design would need even more.

Design Charts in other books may show you even more things. The important thing is always to study a Design Chart carefully.

TO BEGIN: For your bookmark, cut a strip of canvas 4 inches (10 cm) wide and 7½ inches (19 cm) long. Tape the edges. Mark a line down the center track of holes from one end to the other, because you will make the center row of stitches first, along that line.

COLORS:

> Row 1 — yellow
> Rows 2 and 5 — orange
> Rows 3 and 6 — hot pink
> Rows 4 and 7 — red

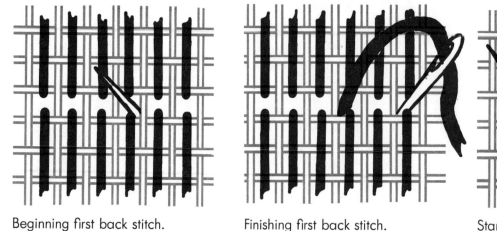

Beginning first back stitch.   Finishing first back stitch.   Starting second back stitch.

TO FINISH THE DESIGN: You probably see canvas threads showing between the rows of Gobelin stitches in this design, because most of its rows are so straight. It is easy to cover them with a Back Stitch. Use red yarn between the red and hot pink rows. Use hot pink yarn between the hot pink and orange rows. Back Stitch shares holes with TWO stitches. Begin (A) by bringing your needle up in the THIRD hole from the end of the design. Follow the chart of Back Stitch steps.

Slanting Stitches

The next stitches slant. They cross the spot at which an up-and-down canvas thread crosses a side-to-side canvas thread. Sometimes slanting stitches are called *diagonal* stitches.

[46]

CHUNKY ELEPHANT

Scotch Squares
Algerian Eyes

Chunky's stitches slant. They are also made in squares.

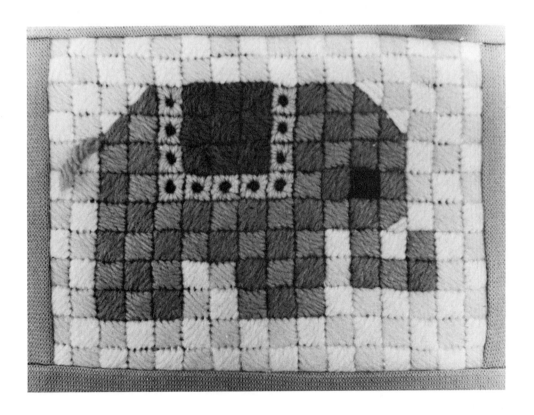

TO BEGIN CHUNKY: Cut a 7-by-9-inch (18 by 23 cm) piece of canvas. Tape the edges. Before you trace the pattern, mark off the canvas in squares.

How to Mark off Canvas for Square Stitches

The square stitches in this book cover 4 canvas threads ACROSS and 4 canvas threads DOWN. They will be easier to stitch if you mark off squares in straight lines, like this:

Next to the left taped edge, draw a light line that runs all the way from the TOP edge to the BOTTOM edge. Keep the line in the same track of threads. Then count 4 threads over from the line you just drew, and draw another up-and-down line in the next track. Keep skipping 4 threads and drawing lines until you reach the RIGHT edge of the canvas.

Now do the same thing for the ACROSS lines. Draw the first one at the top edge of the canvas. As you draw, check to make sure each square contains 4 threads ACROSS and 4 threads UP AND DOWN.

TRACE THE PATTERN: To make sure the square stitches will fit, center Chunky's trunk between 2 of the up-and-down lines you drew. Put his feet on an across line. Use a heavy line to trace, since this outline will often sit on the light lines you used to mark off canvas squares.

[48]

CHUNKY ELEPHANT PATTERN

Trace heavy black lines onto the canvas you marked in squares. Other lines show how to place the pattern on the marked canvas. X marks the first Scotch Square. Dotted squares will be Algerian Eye stitches.

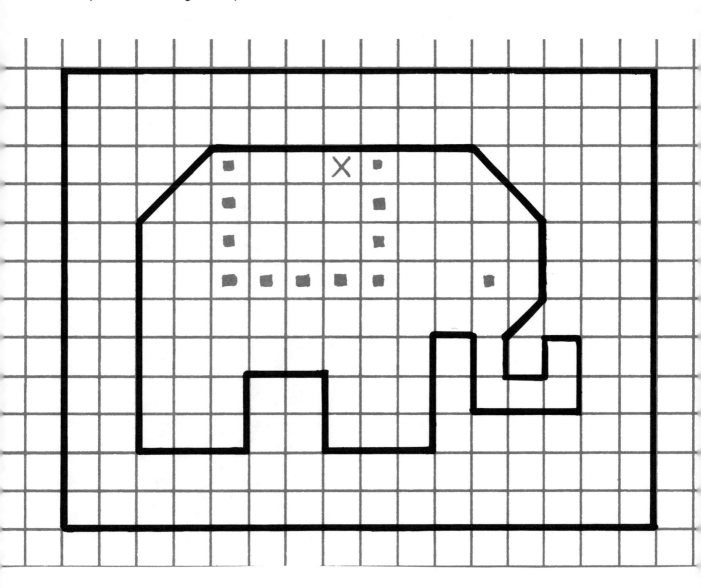

TO STITCH: Choose 1 HOT color, 2 COOL colors, 1 or 2 PALE colors, and white.

Begin with Scotch Squares. First, look at the chart of 1 Scotch Square. Then look at the larger chart of Scotch Squares.

BLANKET: With your hot color, make Scotch Squares in the nine squares that make the middle of Chunky's blanket. Start with the upper right square marked X on the pattern. Next make the middle square in the blanket, and then the lower left square.

In the big chart, do you see how this diagonal row of Scotch Squares you have made is crossed by another diagonal row of squares? Make these. Slant their STITCHES in the opposite direction, too. Keep crisscrossing rows of Scotch Squares until all the blanket's middle is filled.

ONE SCOTCH SQUARE

It is actually 7 slanting stitches.

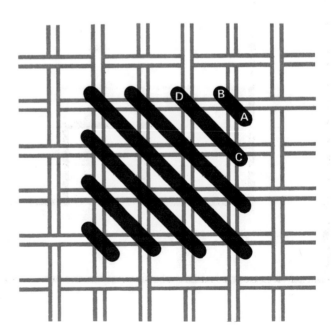

SCOTCH SQUARES

Diagonal rows of squares that slant in one direction (black stitches) are crossed with diagonal rows of squares that slant in the opposite direction (white stitches). Start the second row at A–B.

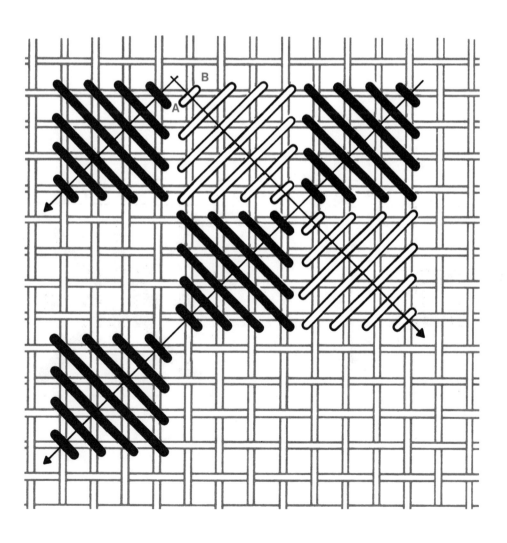

BLANKET BORDER: With a PALE color, make 9 Algerian Eyes. First, push your needle around the edges of the center hole in each square until that hole is a little bigger than the holes around it. See how all 8 stitches in the Algerian Eye begin in that hole? Start by putting your needle up through that center hole. Make the A–B stitch. Make the other stitches in order, clockwise. Start each stitch in the center hole.

SPACE FOR ONE ALGERIAN EYE

Enlarge the center hole.

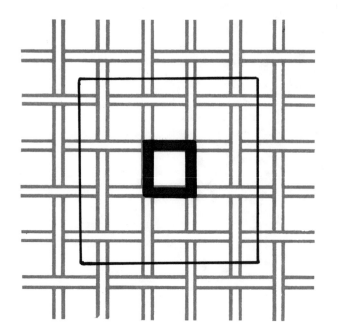

ALGERIAN EYE

All stitches begin in the same hole as A.

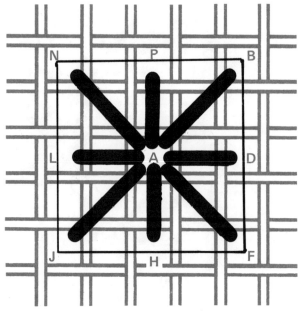

BODY: Use two COOL colors. All the stitches in his body are Scotch Squares. Start with the squares along Chunky's forehead to make a diagonal row of Scotch Squares in one cool color. Cross that row with a row of squares in the other cool color. Keep crisscrossing rows of color.

Along the edges of the body are PARTS of squares to make in Chunky's colors. The other parts of these squares are made in background colors.

EYE: When the row you are making reaches the square that is Chunky's eye, make a black Scotch Square. Or you may prefer to make an Algerian Eye in the color you used for the blanket border.

BACKGROUND: Here you simply finish the design in all one color, or make a checkerboard of Scotch Squares in 2 pale colors, or 1 pale color and white.

TAIL: Anchor a thread under stitches on the back of the canvas. Bring it through to the front. Cut off all but 1 inch (2.5 cm) and leave the tail dangling loose.

Chunky makes a great center for an 11-inch (28 cm) square pillow. Directions for the pillow are in Part Four.

ANNA'S HATBAND
Rice Stitch

To make a hatband like Anna's, you learn the Rice Stitch. This is a thick, puffy square of slanting stitches.

You also follow another Design Chart, which mixes slanting rows of Rice Stitch with slanting rows of Scotch Squares.

TO BEGIN: Cut a strip of canvas 4 inches (10 cm) wide and 2 inches (5 cm) longer than the distance around your hat (about 24 inches [61 cm]). Tape the edges. Choose 3 colors of yarn. Anna chose black, white, and yellow.

MARK CANVAS IN SQUARES: Start by marking a line 1 inch (2.5 cm) from the taped edge from end to end of the long canvas strip. Count over 4 canvas threads and mark a second long line. Mark the third long line 4 canvas threads away from the second, the

fourth long line 4 canvas threads away from the third, and the fifth long line 4 canvas threads away from the fourth. This will make your hatband 16 canvas threads wide. Now, starting 1 inch (2.5 cm) from the end of the canvas, mark crossing lines every fourth thread.

TO STITCH: Study the Design Chart. Start by holding your canvas with the length running from left to right, as in the picture. Make the Scotch Square marked with the big arrow in the upper right-hand square. Use black yarn. Now make the other three black Scotch Squares in this slanting row.

DESIGN CHART

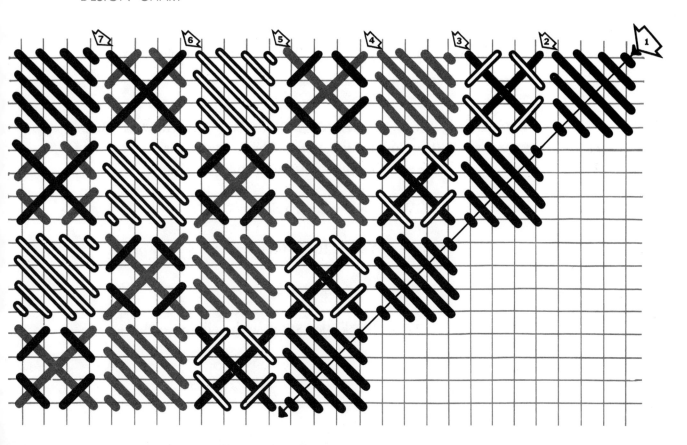

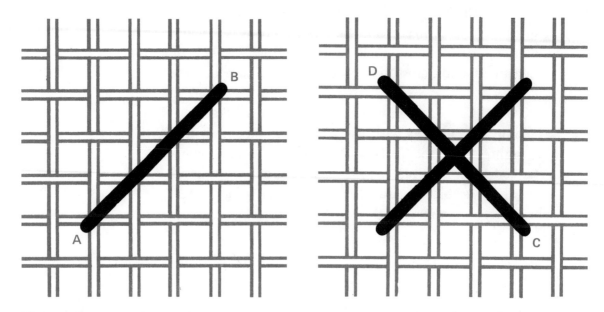

Make a slanting stitch over 4 intersections.

Then cross it with another stitch.

SECOND SLANTING ROW: This row is Rice
Stitch. Follow the Stitch Chart. Make the big crosses
black and the small crossbars white.

ROW 3: Yellow Scotch Squares.

ROW 4: Yellow Rice Stitch with black crossbars.

ROW 5: White Scotch Squares.

ROW 6: Black Rice Stitch with yellow crossbars.

[56]

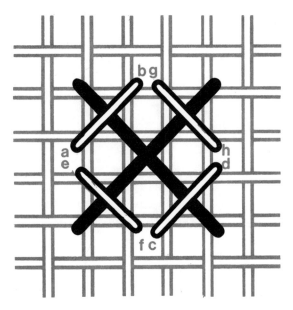

Now, over each arm of the X you
have made, make small crossbars that
cover 2 canvas intersections.

AFTER ROW 6: Start all over with directions for
Row 1 and repeat the other rows in order until the
design is 1 inch (2.5 cm) from the other end of the
canvas. Fill the slanting ends with parts of rows.

To finish your design into a hatband, you will need
an equal length of 2-inch (5 cm) grosgrain ribbon,
felt, or wide tape for a lining. To attach the lining,
follow directions in Part Four. Then put the hatband
on your hat.

If that was fun, make a belt or bookmark with the
same design chart.

FLOWER PATCH

Upright Cross Stitch
Tent Stitch

To make this mini-garden, use the pattern as both pattern and stitch guide. Trace the heavy lines on a 7½-by-7½-inch (19 by 19 cm) square of canvas. Tape the edges.

FLOWER PATCH PATTERN

TO STITCH: Make the shaded sections of the pattern in Upright Cross Stitch. Use yellow in the center of the big flower. Use green in the shaded parts of the small flowers.

Upright Cross is an important stitch because it makes a thick area, but it takes longer than other stitches to make, so it is a good stitch to use in a small area!

LEAVES AND PETALS: All leaves and petals are long Gobelin stitches. Make them in the direction of the arrows on the pattern. Make leaves green. Make petals in 1 or 2 hot colors (strawberry pink, orange, or red).

STEMS: In green, make side-to-side Gobelin stitches that begin and end in the same tracks of canvas holes.

TOP OF SMALL FLOWERS: Make yellow Upright Crosses where you see x's on the pattern.

BACKGROUND: In white or a pale color, do the entire background in Tent Stitch. Start at the upper right-hand corner.

UPRIGHT CROSS
STITCHES

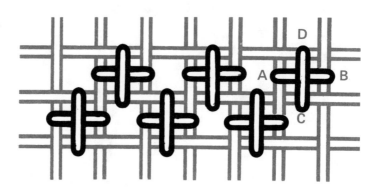

Tent Stitch is the stitch most people learn first and the stitch you will learn last. You might call it the Snail Stitch because it is so very slow. When you hear other people call Tent Stitch such names as "Basketweave," or "Continental," or "Half Cross," they are describing the method and direction of putting stitches into the canvas. We are using the "Continental" method, which is good for outlining shapes and for "signing" larger pieces with your initials. With the Continental method, stitch every other row with the canvas held upside down. Always stitch from right to left. Used in large areas, Tent Stitch will pull your canvas out of shape so that it needs to be blocked. Part Four gives you directions for blocking.

When your Flower Patch is finished, most of the canvas you bought will be used up. If you have cut it carefully, there will be enough left to make your very own design. Part Three tells you how easy that is.

ONE ROW OF TENT STITCH

Start at top right corner of the canvas. Stitch from right to left.

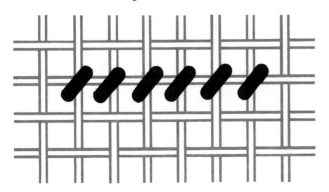

TWO ROWS OF TENT STITCH

Turn canvas upside down to stitch the second row from right to left.

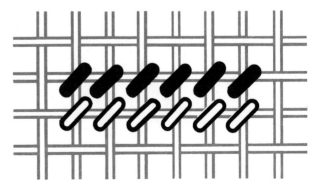

PART THREE

Making Your Own Designs

If you have ever drawn a bird or animal on paper, you can become a designer of needlepoint. After you have read this part and looked at designs made by young designers like these, the rest is easy.

To Begin: Sketch a Design

All you do is cut a square of paper the size you want your finished needlepoint design to be. On it, sketch a bird or animal in pencil. OUTLINE the sketch with your marker, trace it on canvas, choose colors and stitches, and begin to stitch.

JEAN'S OWL

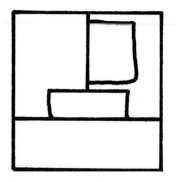

Straight lines alone can be dull.

Slanting lines add interest.

Many shapes are more fun to see.

Where Do Designs Come from?

The best original designs start with something you have seen and enjoyed. These designers sketched birds and animals. They gathered up books and magazines with photographs in them. They looked at birds flying, birds walking, birds sitting on nests. They looked, really looked, at the shapes of animals and saw how shapes changed in various positions. They chose chunky, short-legged animals because these are easier to needlepoint. They drew the whole body, because designs with only heads seldom look good.

Have a happy afternoon sketching birds or animals on your squares of paper, at the zoo, on a farm, or from magazines at home. One of your drawings is certain to be a good first needlepoint design if you sketch only the outline and only the most important details.

Before You Trace, Adjust the Lines

If a sketch seems almost right, changing a line or a shape can make it exactly right. Think of your Smooth Sailor. If all the shapes had been square or round and all the lines up and down, you wouldn't enjoy looking at it. Slanting sails added interesting lines. Straight lines held them in the picture. A round man in a square hat, on a boat with pointed bow and stern, made interesting shapes. Good needlepoint designs have fewer lines than many pictures you draw, but every line has more to do. If you think of these things

[64]

while you sketch, your eyes will tell you when to stop sketching. Then you can needlepoint again!

See how these designers adjusted their sketches?

Dave's penciled bird perched on a limb, but the bird made Dave wonder what it was staring at, out beyond the border. Dave decided to let the bird fly to the ground. To do that, he drew a horizon line higher than the bird's feet and one third of the way up the picture so the bird would have grass to stand in. What sensible bird stands ON a horizon line? To keep the bird busy, Dave added a worm.

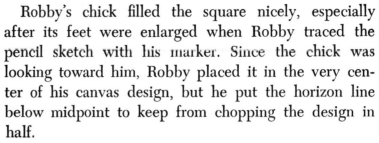

Robby's chick filled the square nicely, especially after its feet were enlarged when Robby traced the pencil sketch with his marker. Since the chick was looking toward him, Robby placed it in the very center of his canvas design, but he put the horizon line below midpoint to keep from chopping the design in half.

Emory's perky squirrel sketch had a lot of dull empty space behind its bushy tail, so Emory moved it back into the design when he traced the squirrel on the canvas.

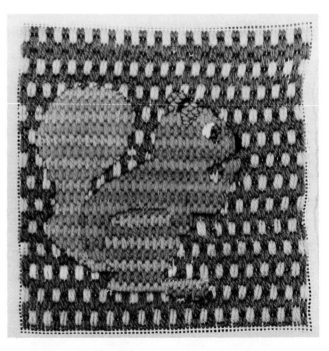

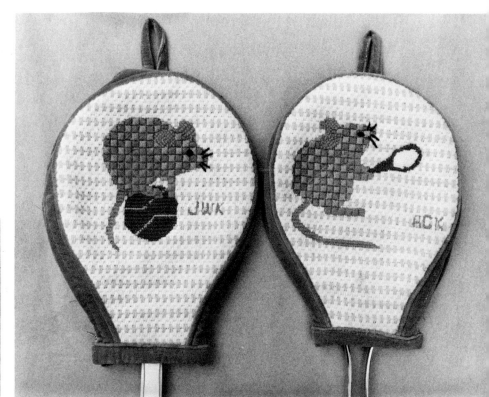

After Julie sketched her mouse, she decided to make a tennis racket cover. What did a mouse have to do with tennis? Nothing much, until Julie stood the mouse on a tennis ball to make the cover. Then Julie put a tennis racket into its paw, and taught her mother some needlepoint stitches, and both of them made racket covers.

When You Trace, Follow Canvas Lines

When you place your paper drawing underneath your canvas square, line up straight lines of the drawing with lines of canvas holes. Sometimes you can make a wing a little bigger or a leg a little straighter. This makes the needlepoint stitches fit better.

Use Bright, Happy Colors

In the forest, animals may be gray and brown, but needlepoint animals need to be bright. Your needlepoint animal can be your favorite bright color, a color that makes you feel good. Then decide what colors to use with the animal. There are many ways to do this.

Think Hot Colors, Cool Colors

Bright reds, oranges, pinks, and yellows are called hot colors. You know why when you look at an orange flame in a fire, or a blazing yellow sun, or zinnias in summer.

Bright blues and greens are called cool colors. You know why when you see a cool blue lake or a leafy green shade tree.

Purple is a mixture of hot red and cool blue. Sometimes it seems hot, sometimes cool, depending on other colors nearby.

When you place hot colors next to cool colors, the

hot colors seem hotter and the cool colors cooler. A red rabbit may hide in cool-color grass, but its hot colors hint that it is about to hop up and find some action.

Whether they are hot or cool, needlepoint animals look better in bright colors, not dull colors.

Colors That Seem Alike Harmonize

If Jimmy had made his red rabbit all red, it would have been a red blob. He used different hot colors, pink and orange, on the legs, so each part can be seen. He still has an all-together rabbit.

Colors That Seem Different Contrast

Jeannie made her butterfly's wings in two yellows, the background in two greens, and the body and wing stripes in red for lots of contrast.

Darks and Lights Make Harmony and Contrast, Too

Elizabeth made light, medium, and dark blue flowers. She made dark green stems and leaves and a yellow-green background. Her pillow has light-and-dark contrast and cool-color harmony. In your design, choose color neighbors according to whether you need contrast or harmony.

Where Do Colors Go?

You can place any color you like anyplace you like it. The trick is to make sure eyes enjoy looking at it.

When eyes see a lot of color in one part of a design, they like to see a little of that same color in another part of the design. A cool-color bird standing on an orange and red ground could have an orange beak.

When eyes see too much of one color, they get bored. When they see two colors mixed together in one large area, they stay interested. You will see some interesting combinations in the designs on the cover of this book.

Test Your Colors

Before you begin stitching, bunch up lengths of the yarn colors you plan to use over each area of your design. If they look good together and give the amount of excitement you want, you are ready to start stitching, IF you have enough yarn of each color to cover the area. You need 1 yard (0.95 m) of yarn for each square inch (6.5 sq. cm) you wish to cover, PLUS a little extra.

When you buy more yarn, get a new supply of the colors you have used in your learning designs. Perhaps you will add lighter and darker values of those same colors. Get an extra supply of your favorite color.

Choosing Stitches

If your fingers have one stitch they like to do best, you can use that one stitch over the entire design. Let colors define the areas. However, it's more exciting to use several stitches.

Look at the stitches you have learned. Let their shapes help you decide.

UPRIGHT GOBELIN makes smooth, even rows and satiny small areas. Choose it when you need rows and small round areas.

PARISIAN STITCH makes a firm, flat pattern. It is good for areas with irregular edges and for backgrounds.

DOUBLE BRICK has a chunky, padded look. It looks important when smaller stitches are used around it, so it is good for important parts of the main design. Double Brick also makes a good background. If you do all the bricks in one color, the area will look smooth. If you do every other row of bricks in a second color, the area will be striped up and down. If you do every third row of bricks in a second color, the area will be spotted.

SINGLE BRICK has a smooth, skinny look. It looks good in less important areas and makes the Double Brick area next to it seem more important. Color changes also make Single Brick change from smooth solids to stripes and spots. The stripes and spots look smaller than in Double Brick.

SCOTCH SQUARES are very, very square, of course, so they fit well in big, square areas.

RICE STITCH and ALGERIAN EYE are also square, but fancier. Use them for show-off areas.

Use UPRIGHT CROSS STITCH and TENT STITCH in small areas. They fit. They are also tedious to use in large areas!

FLAME STITCH can be feathers, grass, mountains, ocean waves, anything that moves up and down. The more colors you include in Flame Stitch, the wilder and wigglier it grows. The only way to quiet it down is to do all the rows in the same color. It is a wonderful, happy stitch that lets your fingers try anything that your eyes want to see.

Teach a Friend

If your needlepoint designs please you, they will please other people too. They will be eager to learn from you. They may even consider you an authority who knows more than you actually know! The designers you have met were teaching stitches to mothers, little brothers, and big sisters while they were still learning stitches themselves. So be a friend!

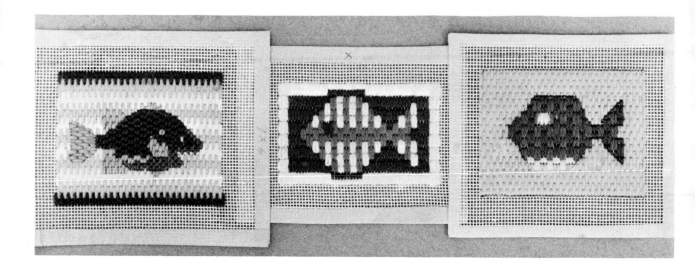

Teach others some stitches. Suggest they choose their own bright colors and change your design to suit themselves. That is how this school of fishes happened.

Here are some other designs our young designers want to share with you and your pupils.

Since you made a Pink Puppy with this Upright Gobelin Stitch, you need no directions to make this landscape.

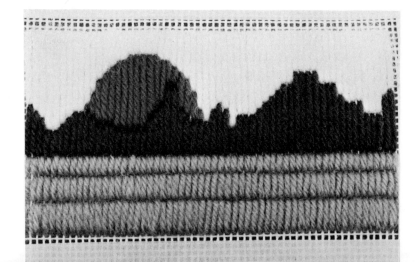

Blair made his flags of long Gobelin stitches for two good reasons. They suited the stripes of the flags, and Gobelin was about the only stitch he knew!

A grownup borrowed an elephant drawn by six-year-old John and made this pillow with stitches she learned from another book. John said you could borrow it, too. Choose your own stitches and colors.

ELEPHANT PATTERN

Do you recognize the stitches in Bryan's Square Bear? The background has 2 rows of white Double Brick, 1 row of yellow, repeated. That turns Double Brick Stitch into dots. Try hot colors on the bear and cool colors on the ground.

SQUARE BEAR PATTERN

A grownup borrowed seven-year-old Tommy's frog sketch, stitched the frog in greens, sat him on an orange lily pad with one leg hanging in a yellow pond, and made a pillow.

FROG PATTERN

If you haven't time to guide your pupils through each learning piece, let them make this pincushion sampler. The borders are rows of Gobelin stitches. Make sure each inside square contains 12 canvas threads in each direction, so there will be room for 9 square stitches at upper right, at center, and at lower left.

Use a different stitch in each square. Use several yarn colors in each square.

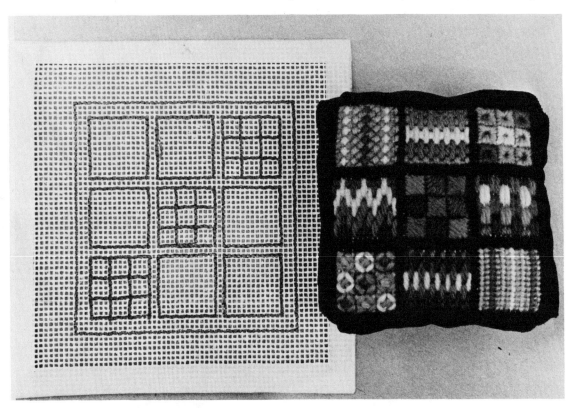

PART FOUR

How to Finish Your Needlepoint

When you put the very last needlepoint stitch in your design, was it finished? Not quite. Those funny unstitched canvas edges are there, and maybe the canvas square is no longer square. What you do about this and how you turn the design into something to use and enjoy is called *finishing*. When finishing is done, the fun of using and sharing your needlepoint starts.

This part of the book tells you some easy ways to finish needlepoint. You can finish many of them without help. To get very special or very difficult pieces finished, ask your needlework shop to have the finishing done. This may be expensive, so try the easy ones yourself.

Getting Your Needlepoint Back to Its Right Shape

All needlepoint pieces will change shape while the stitches are being made. Getting them back to their right shape is called *blocking*.

Luckily, most of the stitches you have used do not pull the canvas sideways. Most of your small designs will be nearly as square and even as they were when you made the first stitch. For these, blocking is easy.

Place the design on the wide end of an ironing board, right side down. Dip a cloth in water, wring it out, and place it over the needlepoint. Press lightly with a hot iron. Next, take the cloth off. To hold it in place, stick rustproof pins through the unworked corners into the ironing board pad. Put the cloth back on. Press again lightly. Leave the canvas in place until you are sure it is dry. The design can then be finished into whatever you plan to make with it.

If Your Needlepoint Is Badly Out of Shape

Slanting stitches sometimes make the whole design lean to one side. When this happens, the design must be dampened all the way through to make the canvas limp. The easy way to do this is to wet an old clean towel, wring out the water, and roll your design up in the towel. Leave it for several hours on a surface that water will not harm. (How about the empty bathtub?)

The next step is to tug at the limp canvas until the design is back to its right shape and to keep it there while it dries.

For a small design, use the wide end of the ironing board and hold it with many pins. For a large design, use a large, flat, wooden surface and rustproof tacks. Plywood is hard to hammer tacks into; choose particle board or other soft wood. Cover the board with an old clean cloth or towel or with plain paper.

1. Lay the design on the covered surface, right side up.
2. Tug the top two corners into place. Hold with tacks.
3. Tug the bottom two corners into place. Measure to see that they are even. Tack into place.
4. The edges between the corners will be drooping. Pull them into place. Hold with tacks.
5. Keep adding tacks until all edges are even.
6. Leave the design in place until its yarn and canvas are dry. Then it is ready to finish.

BLOCK YOUR CANVAS TO ITS CORRECT SHAPE

This design needs to be dampened and blocked.

Get the four corners of the damp design square again.

Get the four edges straight, and let it dry.

How to Keep Your Needlepoint Clean

After your design is blocked, spray the stitches lightly with a fabric protector such as Scotchgard. Let the first light spraying dry. Spray lightly twice more. Let it dry each time.

To Add a Lining

Pockets and other flat pieces need to be lined with cloth. To make a cloth lining, cut a piece of fabric 1 inch (2.5 cm) longer and 1 inch (2.5 cm) wider than the needlepoint design.

1. With an iron, press under ½-inch (1.3 cm) hems all around the edge of the lining. Put the lining aside.
2. Peel off the masking tape from the canvas edges of your needlepoint design. With scissors, trim off all but ½ inch (1.3 cm) of the unstitched canvas edge, if there is more margin.
3. Fold under the ½-inch (1.3 cm) canvas edges so that only the stitches show on the right side. To keep the edges under, use a needle and regular sewing thread to make large stitches. Let these stitches go through the canvas edge and catch some of the canvas threads beneath the yarn. Take care not to catch the fronts of the stitches.
4. Pin the back side of the lining to the back side of the needlepoint design. With sewing needle and

thread, join the lining edge to the design edge. Use tiny stitches. Try to make stitches that do not show. Also, when the stitches are made, make sure the lining keeps the canvas threads from peeking through.

Sometimes you can use grosgrain ribbon or felt to line a small needlepoint design. To line a strap or skinny design with grosgrain ribbon, buy ribbon the same width as your design. Cut it 1 inch (2.5 cm) longer than the design. Press under ½ inch (1.3 cm) at each end. The sides of the ribbon will not fray, so they do not have to be turned under. Put the pieces together with tiny stitches.

Cut a felt lining exactly the same size as the design. Do not turn under the edges. Put the pieces together with tiny stitches.

A lining should match one of the yarn colors in the design.

HOW TO ADD A LINING

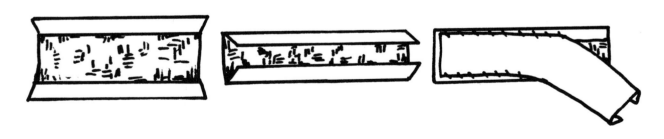

How to Make Crafts Projects of Your Designs

Now that you know how to block your design and attach a lining, about all you need to learn is the proper size and shape for new projects. This will help you make a favorite design more than once and use it to make different things.

A square design like Smooth Sailor can be a picture or a pocket or the middle of a pillow. A rectangle like Tricky Fish can be a picture or the middle of a pillow. A bookmark design can be made longer for a camera strap, belt, or guitar strap. Three straps can become straps for a luggage rack.

You will remember, of course, to cut canvas larger than the design so it will have margins all around. Also remember to turn under the canvas edges and to make cloth linings at least ½ inch (1.3 cm) larger all around.

Finished pieces should be these sizes and made into projects this way:

BELT: 1 to 3 inches wide (2.5 to 7.5 cm), depending on the design's width, and 4 inches (10 cm) longer than the waist it is to fit. TO FINISH: Line it (see page 86). Ask a shoe repairman to add a buckle and grommets for holes.

BOOKMARK: 1½ to 2 inches (4 to 5 cm) wide; 4 to 6 inches (10 to 15 cm) long. TO FINISH: Center the design on a length of grosgrain ribbon the same width as the design and 4 inches (10 cm) longer. Stitch them to-

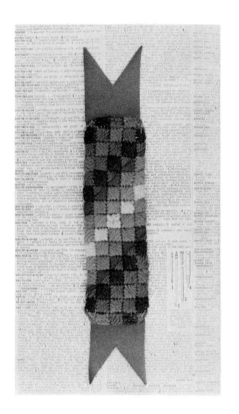

gether with tiny stitches, or use a sewing machine. Notch the ends of the ribbon.

EYEGLASSES CASE: 3 by 13 inches (7.5 by 33 cm). To hold larger glasses: 3½ by 14 inches (9 by 35.5 cm). TO FINISH: First, line the strip (see page 86). Then fold the strip in the middle with the open ends together. Hold the folded piece in place with pins. Make tiny stitches to close the sides of the case. Let some of the stitches catch the canvas threads beneath the yarn.

GUITAR STRAP: 2 to 4 inches (5 to 10 cm) wide; 42 inches (107 cm) long. TO FINISH: Line with cloth or ribbon (see page 86). Have a shoe repairman add a grommet 1 inch (2.5 cm) away from each end. The grommet should be centered on the width of the strap. Put a shoestring through each grommet. Tie the shoestrings to the guitar.

HATBAND: 2 inches (5 cm) wide (or as wide as your strap design); 22 to 24 inches (56 to 61 cm) long (or the distance around your hat). TO FINISH: Line it (see page 86). Put it around your hat. Sew the ends together with tiny stitches.

LUGGAGE RACK STRAPS: Make three strap designs just alike. Each strap should be 2 inches (5 cm) wide and 22 inches (56 cm) long. TO FINISH: Line each strap (see page 86). Use a hammer and short nails with big heads on them to attach the straps to a luggage rack.

PICTURE: When you have blocked your design, take it to a framer. Have the framer add a mat and a frame.

PILLOW: You decide what size your pillow should be. Choose a design that is a square or a rectangle. The pillow can be the same size as the design, or a small design can be the middle of a big pillow.

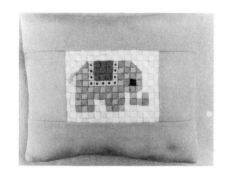

FOR A SMALL PILLOW: Your design will be the front of the pillow. Cut a pillow back from velveteen or corduroy. Make it ½ inch (1.3 cm) larger all around than the needlepoint. Pin the right side of the design to the right side of the back. On a sewing machine, with the design side on top, stitch just inside

HOW TO TURN A SMALL DESIGN INTO A LARGE PILLOW

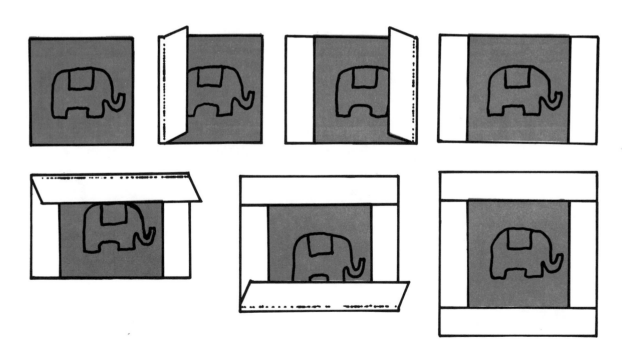

the edges of the design, so that the machine thread is catching a tiny part of the outside yarn stitches. Stitch all 4 sides, but leave a 3-inch (7.5 cm) opening at the bottom.

Now trim away all but ½ inch (1.3 cm) of the canvas that is outside the machine stitching. Turn the pillow right side out. Through the opening you left, stuff polyester fiberfill into the pillow until it is nice and fat. Then turn the seam part of the opening inside. Pin the front and back of the opening together. Make tiny stitches to close the opening. Now you have a small pillow.

FOR A LARGE PILLOW: Follow the drawings to "frame" your design with cloth. From corduroy or velveteen, cut the two side flaps. On a sewing machine, stitch them to the sides of the design. Then cut the top and bottom flaps and stitch them in place. That makes the front of your large pillow. TO FINISH: Cut a pillow back from the same fabric used to make the flaps. It should be exactly the same size as the front of the pillow. Follow directions for a small pillow to put the pieces together and stuff the pillow.

PINCUSHION: Choose a square design from 3 by 3 inches (7.5 by 7.5 cm) to 6 by 6 inches (15 by 15 cm) in size. TO FINISH: Follow directions for making a small pillow.

RUG FOR A DOLLHOUSE: Make your design a size that fits the floor of the dollhouse. TO FINISH: When the edges are turned under, cut a lining of felt the same size as the design. Use glue or tiny stitches to put the felt lining on the design.

TENNIS RACKET COVER: Before you make the needlepoint, make a pattern. Get a big piece of paper. Put your tennis racket on it. Trace around the head of the racket and down 1 inch (2.5 cm) of the handle. Next, draw a line that follows the same shape, 1 inch (2.5 cm) outside of the traced line, all the way around. The outside line will be your pattern. Trace that line onto a rectangle of canvas. Allow for 1-inch (2.5 cm) margins at the widest parts of the outline. Now center your design inside the racket shape and trace it on the canvas. Now the design and background are ready to needlepoint.

Finishing a tennis racket needlepoint design is not easy. Ask your needlework supply shop to have the finishing done for you.

What Else?

Do you feel adventurous, now that you have done several designs and stitches on No. 10 canvas? Here are some tips that make it easy for you to experiment.

Other Sizes of Canvas

No. 14 canvas, which many people like best, has 14 holes to the inch (2.5 cm). Using it takes greater patience and a smaller needle. There are many smaller-holed canvas sizes. It helps to remember that their numbers mean the number of canvas holes or threads across 1 inch (2.5 cm) of canvas. The higher the number, the more stitches you'll need.

More fun and faster than other canvas is No. 5, with big holes. Try one of the Design Charts from this book on No. 5 canvas. It will be FOUR TIMES as large as it was on No. 10 canvas. Carol felt super-adventurous. She put some extra peaks in Flame Stitch and put the design on No. 5 canvas. With bigger yarn and a huge needle, she finished her large pillow in just a few days. For pieces this large, allow 1½-inch (4 cm) canvas margins.

Washable Needlepoint

If you feel very brave, try this way of putting washable needlepoint stitches directly into washable fabric, like the design on Jim's jeans pocket. The canvas becomes a stitch guide only.

Trace the design on the canvas, as usual. With sewing needle and thread, use big stitches to hold the needlepoint canvas on top of the fabric you wish to trim. Instead of yarn, use washable embroidery floss to make the needlepoint stitches. Make sure each stitch goes through both the canvas and the fabric behind it. Stitch the design only. Leave the background unstitched. When all the stitches are in place, pull out the UP-AND-DOWN canvas threads, one at a time. Then pull out all the ACROSS canvas threads, one at a time. This will leave the stitches in the fabric.

Try this first on a flat piece of fabric. If, later, you do a jeans pocket, make sure none of the stitches catch the seat of the jeans behind the pocket.

Happy Stitching!

It is time for this book to end, but it is not time for you to stop enjoying needlepoint. Let it be a happy part of the rest of your life. If you want to try other methods, go to your library. There you will find dozens of good needlepoint books filled with ways to use other sizes and kinds of canvas and yarn, with patterns that have become a part of history and are fun to re-create, and with hundreds more stitches. Try as many as you wish, but always remember this:

The kind of needlepoint you already know guarantees you a joyous freedom that many people who work only from needlepoint kits never learn, even though they make beautiful things. Somewhere inside every person is an artist. Through your kind of needlepoint, the artist in you comes out and shares happiness with the rest of the world. Keep that happening in your needlepoint and in all the other fun things you do. You are a very special person, and the world needs you because you are.